# DON'T LOVE ME LIKE THIS

## ANJALI GUPTA

*To all the lovers out there.*

# Contents

# 1. Life before I met you.

*My heart doesn't feel anything but pain*
*I let my heart get hurt until my tears rain*
*I wanna die but killing myself feels like a crime*
*Pain has been my lover for a long time*
*It's filled in my bone*
*It never leaves me alone*
*It's there when I'm awake*
*It's there when I'm sleeping*
*It's there when I laugh*
*It's there when I'm weeping*
*It hugs my heart so tightly*
*So tightly that I can't breathe*
*I like my pain now*
*Cuz I know it'll never leave*

Crush...

# 2. Blush Is In The Air

*What's this rush in my heart?*
*It's something I have never felt*
*Am I getting a crush on a guy?*
*A guy I have never met*

*"Why don't you send a snap of your face?",*
*I want to ask you as my heart craves*
*I want to say I'm not interested in seeing the videos of ur friends*
*having fun*
*I'm interested to see you laughing behind the camera of pun*
*I heard your voice and I want to tell you I wanna hear it all my*
*life*
*What if you become my man*
*And I, your wife*

*You followed me on insta*
*And here I am*
*Diving into your profile with a stalking passion*
*Oh you look so kind*
*I notice your bad sense of fashion*
*And now I'm shopping for your clothes in my mind*

.....

*Oh I am so silly*
*But you*
*You are worth being silly for*

*You turn out to be my roommate's friend*
*Sitting in the same room as me*
*I haven't thought about you in a while*
*Maybe for me, pain is the only key*
*You are laughing with your guys*
*I'm lost in my own disguise*
*But when we went out for a treat*
*Oh when you held my hand to help me cross the muddy street*
*I forbid myself to feel my heart getting rushed*
*It's just a crush, I tell myself*
*And crushes get crushed*

*Sitting with ur friend circle, I can't stop looking at you*
*We order the same pizza, your friend is eating yours too*
*I'm thinking of giving you my pizza slice*
*Would you take it? Or would you just roll your eyes?*
*You're going back to your place and my heart is breaking like*
*glass toys*
*You offer a handshake from a moving bike and I miss it, my*
*mind says STAY AWAY FROM BOYS*

*Yes*
*My mind doesn't want you in my story*
*And my heart is scared too*
*I don't want to fall in love again*
*But I'm unable to resist you*
*No*
*It's just a crush*
*But*
*We meet again and you fix my phone*
*I look at you and my heart is blown*
*U text me, I allow myself to uncloak*
*And now we are cracking an inside joke*

*.....*

*Do you like me?*
*I really don't wanna ask*
*Why can't my heart just do it's biological task?*
*Sharing reels with each other, maybe we are now semifriends*
*Our story has started, let's see how it ends*

*You are sending me hints and I think you like me*
*I don't know how to tell you how much you entice me*
*No matter who I'm with, I always think about you*
*It makes me wonder if you are getting butterflies too*
*Day dreaming about you is my new hobby*
*I've kissed you infinite times in my heart's lobby*
*But no, I can't let my guards down*
*I have a disturbing past, and I don't wanna drag you into my*
*trauma town*

*My heart is racing as you are coming to talk about your feelings*
*I want to keep you in my life forever*
*But if you find out about my scary dealings*
*Will you accept me in your heart? The answer is never*

*You come into my room and my heart skips a beat*
*How can a guy look so charmingly neat?*
*I tell you about my demons and my scars*
*That if you let me into your life, you'll have to deal with my*
*dreadful wars*
*I'm ready to see you make excuses and leave*
*But you listen about every nonexistent things I believe*
*Your eyes meet mine and ohh I drowned in those brown eyes*
*My stomach has gotten the whole town's butterflies*
*You said you want to be with me and asked for a chance*
*I'm scared as hell but I'll let my heart dance*

Love...

# 3. I Love You More

*I have this wish of drowning in your eyes on a coffee date*
*You ask to take me for a coffee and I wonder if it's fate*
*I'm all ready but you are late*
*Are you with someone else? Am I just your bait?*
*No I can't let the poison of my past ruin our heavenly bond*
*With you, I wanna jump into the cupid pond*
*So I'll let aside my doubts*
*Won't ask you for your whereabouts*
*But know that if you hurt me I'm over*
*So will you kill my heart or keep it safe forever?*

*We talk every day*
*And each day is getting smaller*
*I don't know how you do this bae*
*But the love bug in my heart is getting taller*
*You live just a little far but it feels like a thousand-mile*
*I hate waiting for the weekends to see your radiant smile*
*I've fought alone every second and I'm tired of this nightmare of*
*a life*
*But you make me feel less lonely, you make me feel like I'm*
*already your wife*
*You have entered my frozen world like a ray of sunshine*
*Let's make our lives full of cute dates, maybe some pizzas and red*
*wine?*

*How do you carry such a positive aura in a world full of lies?*
*All I Know is that when you are not close my heart cries*
*I want you around all the time*
*It's like you carry a magical thyme*
*I'm captivated by your love's chime*
*Do my poems even rhyme?*

*I didn't know this is how true love feels*
*For you, I'm totally head over heels*
*You are so beautiful, oh my god your eyes*
*So full of love, they contain a million skies*
*I could fly in them for hours*
*I'll look at you until my heart devours*
*This love is spreading through each and every cell*
*I wish you stay, I hope I'm not just getting some stories to tell*

*.....*

*My existence has been like a torture tale*
*But you are making my cheeks red from pale*
*I'll hold onto the hope of endless happiness with you*
*Do you want to stay with me till the end or are you gonna break*
*my heart too?*

*I've been a warrier*
*Fighting alone my battles of mind*
*Until you became my saviour*
*I got no help from the human kind*
*You came like a miracle*
*Pushing the biggest obstacle*
*Finally I can rest, finally I can walk blind*
*You are the soulmate I thought I'd never find*

*Now when I start losing*
*When my monsters fight*
*You save me from dying*
*You hold me so tight*
*I swear if your love is endless*
*If you'll always be in my sight*
*I'm ready to fight with the darkness*
*As you are my light*

*I'm an anxiety bomb and you are the technician*
*Your love filled look calms me like a magician*
*I've tried healing activities like a million times*
*But with you, this process sublimes*
*I still see my monsters and they keep tormenting me*
*But with you, I feel free*

*.....*

*Free of fighting alone*
*Free of feeling helpless*
*Free of always being in the danger zone*
*Free of seeing this pain as something endless*
*Free of the burden of the dark world that I've known*
*With you, I'm transitioning into a gem stone*

*I'm diving into your soul and see you've got some scars too*
*I get onto treating those, I never want to see you feeling blue*
*I don't know how but your pain hurts me more than my own*
*You are the beauty of life I was never shown*
*I wanted to die but now I wanna live for you*
*I intend to stick with you forever like a glue*

*Healing each other, we'll live a happy life full of love*
*We'll be old together and sit in the backyard looking at the stars*
*above*
*I'll be a writer working from home*
*When you'll come back you'll find me writing a poem*
*I'll write love poems about us till the end*
*This spark will be there no matter how much time we spend*
*We'll be those old love birds new generation will call couple goals*
*We'll never let go of each other even in the world of souls*

*All these days with you feel like living in a dream*
*We decide to live together and oh my god I feel like I'll scream*
*I'll tell everyone how much I'm in love with this stupid ethereal*
*man*
*We'll make this room a home, we'll make it as beautiful as we*
*can*
*This feels like a whole new chapter*
*We'll fill this one with love and laughter*
*I'm thinking I should start a journal*
*As it should be written how our love is eternal*

*Putting fairy lights in our room*
*I can picture you as my groom*
*We'll have a small marriage on a mountain cliff*
*Ohh we'll get a puppy who'll sniff, sniff, sniff*
*I print our photos and stick them to the lights*
*Living together, we'll learn cooking tasty delights*
*No matter how much I decorate this place it's your presence that*
*makes it feel like home*
*Perhaps someday we'll elope and start living in Rome*
*As I'm lost in the dreamy thoughts*
*I notice you are looking at me with that majestic smile*
*My eyes start wandering to different spots*
*But my heart is dancing somewhere on the bathroom tile*

*Everything is falling in place*
*Together, we are so happy*
*Our relationship is moving at a fast pace*
*But why move slow when you meet someone equally crazy*
*We are so in love we are so attached*
*It feels like now all our wounds are patched*
*But my monsters are still there always bleeding me with swords*
*You clean my blood and promise to never leave me alone from*
*this moment onwards*

*We can't fight each other's battles*
*But we save us from going to our dooms*
*We can't stop the world from leaving cuts on us*
*But we heal each other's wounds*
*Every time we get a burn*
*We feed medicine with spoons*
*And if the world ever breaks us*
*We'll meet in each other's glooms*

*I can't believe how much I love you*
*It's like you are residing in my soul*
*Ohh to be stuck forever in a hug with you*
*I wish time was in our hands to control*
*Time flies by and we have to go our separate ways*
*Long distance is tough but it's not a distance if your heart is*
*where my heart stays*
*We hug each other and cry until I have to leave*
*You promise you are just a call away and I let my heart believe*

*You write me a letter and give me while saying goodbyes*
*I take it from your hands with tears in my eyes*
*I keep reading your love again and again in order to stay alive*
*Away from you, I'm scared I won't survive*

Hurt...

# 4. Destined To Stay Broken

*It's not going as you said it will*
*You don't call me and I'm just bleeding with the quill*
*I hate this distance, not the road's but our heart's*
*We are drifting away and I feel this is how my end starts*

. . . . .

*Days pass and every day I miss you more*
*You spend your time with other people and leave me crying alone*
*on the floor*
*I feel like I don't recognize you anymore*
*Do you have any idea how you are hurting me to my core?*

*You used to make me calm*
*Now I stay anxious all day*
*My wounds are bleeding but you are not coming to apply the*
*balm*
*I plead you to call me, I have so much to say*
*I suffer alone unable to breathe*
*My wounds depend on you to treat*
*I call you asking for help but you say you'll talk to me later*
*You are busy with your family exploring a crater*
*I keep suffering for an hour with no sign of your care*
*You call me after 5 hours, finally got some time to spare*

*I pick your call and you sound casual*
*I tell you how I suffered and you feel so cruel*
*You apologize and give reasons that are not valid*
*After suffering so much, your excuses burn me like acid*
*You promise it'll never happen again*
*I can't stop crying, you say my tears causes you pain*
*I had promised myself I'll never let another guy treat me bad*
*But oh I'm in love, I'll let myself become mad*

*I'm losing the fight with my monsters*
*I really need your help*
*You told me we are life partners*
*Then why am I choking myself?*
*You are not there for me*
*Why did you make all those big promises?*
*I've got ghosts around no one can see*
*I'm still alone and it turns out I'm not a person someone misses*

*Yet again I'm crying on a call with you*
*Asking you to love me properly*
*You say you love me more than I love you*
*But I'm waiting for you to show this love you talk about endlessly*
*It has been 10 minutes and your parents call you to have ice-*
*cream*
*You leave me in pain again, no matter how much I scream*
*.....*
*How can my value drop from life to less than a frozen dessert?*
*I'm tired of my existence now, I just keep getting hurt*

*You say you suffer from a problem*
*You say you just can't say no to people*
*But you say no to me all the time*
*You bleed my heart poking a needle*
*When you see you are coming as a bad guy*
*You start lying and break me like a toy*
*I know this relationship has ended but what do I tell my heart?*
*You keep saying it won't happen again and I just hope it to be a*
*new start*

*We are together for the world but I've lost the feeling of getting*
*loved*
*I'm trying to get you back but we are just getting shoved*
*Our bond was so beautiful, your change came as a shock*
*I'm full of agony but I don't have you to talk*
*It's like I'm standing in front of the door waiting for your knock*
*But I'm just hearing the tik tok of the clock*

*You once made me feel like flying through the sky*
*Oh you were such a cutiepie*
*No matter what happened, you always had something sweet to*
*say*
*Maybe that's why you always took my breath away*
*You still take my breath away and do everything it takes*
*Earlier in the form of butterflies, now in the form of heartbreaks*

*I had fallen for your autumn eyes*
*I didn't know they carry countless lies*
*You love me in words but hurt me in actions*
*And I keep staying in the pain of my heart's contractions*
*I can't believe you jumped from my day dreams to scary*
*nightmares*
*My soul starts shivering from even your harmless actions but who*
*cares?*
*I can fight with the world all my life*
*But I'm tired of fighting you*
*I hope you can see I'm stabbed with your knife*
*But you act like you don't have any clue*

*I was walking in deep darkness, and you came like a streetlight*
*in between*
*I tried to hold on to that light forever*
*But if we get depended on it for a long time, even the light gets*
*irritated and starts flickering*
*Now I'm back to roaming in the darkness that ends never*
*I'm lost in the world in search of the same light*
*But maybe I won't find it, I'm just destined to lose in this fight*

*Staying in this darkness feels like eternity*
*I have no idea you now reside in which city*
*We still talk sometimes but we don't know each other*
*I stay alive to listen to your voice, I'm still your lover*
*I keep losing my wars, I think I should just die*
*But I want to live a life where you love me again, so for now I'll*
*just cry*
*You hurted me so bad, your knife had the best sharpness*
*And here I am waiting for you sitting in the darkness*
*I don't know if I have anything left in me*
*I don't know if you intend to pull me into the light*
*I don't know if you'll bring your love key*
*I don't know if you'd want to be with me in this fight*
*But if you ever find my track*
*If you ever come back*
*Don't just love me in words but love me in your actions*
*Show me I mean something to you, make me feel like I'm not*
*just one of your distractions*
*Love me like you've fallen in love*
*Love me like I'm your bliss*
*Love me like I'm your dove*
*But don't love me like this…*

# The End ???

What do you think?

# 5. Your Story

*If you have a story to tell, write it here and share with me on my
instagram: _withlove.anjali_
Awaiting to enter your magical world...*